My Heart's Key

Constance Ffrench

iUniverse, Inc.
New York Bloomington

My Hearts Key

iUniverse books may be ordered through booksellers or by contacting:

iUniverse
1663 Liberty Drive
Bloomington, IN 47403
www.iuniverse.com
1-800-Authors (1-800-288-4677)

ISBN: 978-1-4401-2004-6 (sc)
ISBN: 978-1-4401-2005-3 (ebook)

Library of Congress Control Number: 2009923525

Printed in the United States of America

iUniverse rev. date: 2/06/2009

Touch of a Lady

Passions so tender that makes me surrender.
Passions long lasting that is what I like to remember.
A little lady so passionate, for I conceive, I am.
A night under dimmed light, locks his chest tight.
One swing of my hip makes my man so randy.
With a whisper, proclaims I am sweet like candy.

Free Your Voice

Unblock your mind and free your voice.

Roar out lioness,
Let your voice be heard.

Let it rumble from your stomach,
Like the ever-ready volcano raring to explode.
Turn up its volume to the highest peak of its point.

Then stand and wait for....

Wait for the shakes and jerks it produces.
The acknowledgment and respects it demands,

Then boom…!

Open your mouth let free your voice. Let its tone burn through their hearts like the lava that spills uncontrolled,
Furthermore, its ashes that wither even the toughest of stone.

Then sit back and view….

View the atmosphere you caused.
Delight yourself in their respect and awareness of you.

The girl they knew, with no voice.

You are an Angel

Petals of roses aren't sweeter like you are,
Your smile glues broken hearts.
Clowns in a mask, aren't funnier than you are,
Your laugh softens souls so hard.
You are my Angel in disguise,
That with no doubt is heavenly bliss.

Through a Smile

The smile on my face is not one of joy, but pain and hurt, the worst of all.
The mouth that widens on my face is my shield to protect me Against you who hurt me.
The smile on my face, not all defused sadness but most:
90% of a hundred, which leaves 10% of joy; so you see not a lot for a smile.
The smile on my face protects my brain from the ticks and tocks of mental strain.
The smile on my face, it warms your heart, but tricks your brain from knowing that my heart is glum.
The smile on my face for many years has spoken thousands of words, but only in whispers just for my ears.
The smile on my face has fooled many but not all.

Through a Child's Eyes

In the blink of an eye, my world shattered like a glass broken in a
million pieces.
Why does it have to be like this?
My world crumbled and froze in time.
Why has this happened? Is it due to me...?

If I were not born, would things be good then?
If I were not born, would this world be a better place for you?
Why do you show such anguish?
Why do you show such misery?
Why are things not brighter, why does it have to be so grey?

When I think of the past, the good times we had.
I used to be smaller and inexpensive as you say,
We were a family. Carefree and strong, what went wrong?

I wish I were smaller, I wish I would shrink.
I am a burden on you, a despicable speck, I am sorry for you.
I am sorry for your grief, I am sorry to make you spend for not one,
But two.

Riddles

Riddles of food, are like jingles in the ears of boys.
Riddles of grime, nothing is worse, that is such a crime.
Riddles that end with red, bores me to bed.
Riddles of pearls, target only girls.
Riddles of sweet nothings, written cleverly to delight.
Riddles all around, half a dozen sold for a pound.
Riddles of the witch, are forever there to make him rich.
Riddles of making out…
Forgive me, my ink has run out.

When the Time is Right

This is not farewell or goodbye,
Only see you soon, when the time is right.
Your visit here in this pass-through world has ended…
It is now time for you to move on, to your father's place.

A place where the brightness of the sun dazzles,
Furthermore, the freshness of the wind sends thrills to all mankind
from head to toe.

A place where man and even the wildest of all beasts sit reasoning,
On the other hand, entertaining themselves with the simplest of
things, may it be checkers or a game of hide and seek.

There, you will be at peace.
You will reunite with your creator. The maker and shaper of you
When you were a visitor at this place we call home.

Therefore, for now wish us well, allow us time to grieve…
You left an empty space in our hearts…

For sure, that space will refill with happy memories of you.
Our hearts will regain their shape.
You have meant different things to us all….
Whatever they may be, today we are here as one.
To see you go on, to your father's house.

You will not be forgotten, but laid to rest,
When the time is right, and move on we must, we will… Meet again.

I Understand

For months I cried,
For years I mourned,
I was an empty shell that walked on the earth.

My heart was yanked, its strings detached.
Why did you leave?

My arms ached, trying to stretch for you
...You were gone.

I needed your arms to feel safe again,
I needed you to tell me you loved me still.

I missed your smile and the jokes you told,
I missed that I was no longer daddy's "Darling Bear".

Now I have grown and learnt to understand,
That your pains, and aches, you could take no more!

You had to go to get some rest, and in my heart,
I wish you best.

Listen out for me and hear my cries,
I am your child so protect me...

Where are You?

The ache in my heart… so strong I want to tear it free.
The voices in my head… so loud I want to hear them no more.
Nevertheless, I am stuck!
What can I do?

I am ravaged in distress; I cannot find my way to success.
Despite all my efforts, I am standing still.
Where is my chariot to whisk me forward?

I am blinded by fog, with no torch at my reach,
I need help to move me on my way.
I am desperate and dismayed.

Where are you God? I call out to you.

You blessed me with life, but no money to live.
I want not for much, but I cannot do with nothing at all.

Like Sweets They Are

Other women's men are like candy, some hard, some soft, some sweet and some bitter.
There are also the ones that stain,
The ones that are chewy, at the same time sticky.
Now they are the men you need to keep your hands off.

As hard as it is, you must, must keep your hands off. They start off sweet-talking, with a dash of a tingle that will blow your top off.
A little squeeze here and there,
Giving you mind-blowing experiences,
So that you cannot put them down,
However, put them down you must, they are not yours.

The longer you keep them, the harder it is to let go,
The harder it gets to let go, the more bitter life will seem.

My Sweet Prince

My sweet Prince, O how fulfilled I am. The sweet times
The happy times, the sad times, the horrid times,
The rougher things become the stronger we are. Fruits of the
Womb, how blessed we are. Not one, but four, a gift
From God we receive,
You are my sun, my rain, my wish star in the night sky.
How warm I feel, when I gaze into your glittering eyes.
You are my voice when I am stuck for words.
My night light, when I need to rest.
You are my Prince, I am your Princess, you are my Lion.
Moreover, I am your Lioness.
The band of gold that keeps us forever, shows eternity,
We shall stay together.

To Me You are Flawless

No light is brighter than you are,
No glitters are shinier than you are,
The sun cannot beat your heat,
Even the rainbow is dimmer than you are.
To me, you are flawless.

Your beauty is not just in my eyes,
Your persona is cheeky and bright.
Your heart is bigger than the world.
To me, you are flawless.

You brighten my day with your laughter and wits,
I miss you when you are not around.
You have no replacements.
To me, you are flawless.

Always on the move
There are no wrongs with you.
Always high in the sky,
Even gravity can't bring you down.
To me, you are flawless.

Your love is for all, big and small,
Your critiques are without prejudice.
You are a five star wonder,
Furthermore, to me, you are flawless.

Trapped

As worthless as she feels, he is there to make her feel worse. As morning breaks he awakens with vexation just at the sight of her. She lies in their bed with fear and misery of being with him, but there is no door to let her out.
She feels trapped. By a monster that gets pleasure from striking her with lashes from his leather belt, there is no escape for her!
She is on the edge. God help her, for he is killing her in silence. Her body is sore from his vigorous lashes and her brain hurts. He twists and turns his words so that she is not sure of reality anymore. She tries to fight his words, but dares not fight against the lashes that bruise her naked body. God help her, she feels trapped. By a beast that wants her not… there is no way out! She is suffocating, breathless and paltry.
She feels lost not understanding why she cannot leave. She is his for life, if she does not break free.
How can one break free?
What can she do to break this spell of wickedness?

Hard Life

I have lived to know a life of hardship and pain,
Not a friendly face around, but only God by my side.

A nameless friend, who I looked up to and was always there for,
denied me of her friendship when I was so sorely at a time of need.

My heart overfilled with anger at this excuse for a friend, ready to explode like a bottle of fizzy which has been shaken a thousand times over.

My eyes watered like a runny tap with no end to its flow, for I was in a house surrounded by ill-headed people and starvation.

Days upon days with nothing but buttered toast and sweetened water. Without money, I had to make do. Not only was I starving for food, but also for clarity, to remind me of my sanity.

I fell at the mercy of desperation.

I was losing my sanity in this world I hated and loved all at once.
I was losing it, but I did not quite lose it.

I was safe, my heart emptied and my eyes dried because I have faith and a soul capable of remarkable forgiveness.

Sentence

I was a prisoner in my house.
You sentenced me to death with the strength and power
Of the words you spoke.
You judged me harshly and broke my pride.
My charge was I, the person I am.

Between minutes, your lyrical melody that melted away,
My blues turned to poison arrows and crushed me whole.

....you damaged me.

My broken parts could hold no more, so,
I prayed to God for a room of faults, to put away
The rest of me.

When in Need

Why turn him away when he needs us?
A bunch of hypocrites is what some of us are.
We mostly know him when things are bad,
We mostly know him when we are sad,
We mostly know him when we are in pain,
We mostly know him when we have something to gain.
We mostly know him when our bank balance prints nil,
We mostly know him when we are ill.

He does not turn away, or tell us to take a pill,
He is always there for us, and that is with no lie.
Therefore, we should seek him, even when we are high.

Days with no End

Days with no end, morning where are you?
He has gone and I am all alone, what aches I have in my bones.
The kids are crying, needing me to hold.
I feel desperate and rejected, cannot hold up on my own.
Now my kids feel alone.
I cannot let them down. I have to uplift myself.
Show them that I am here not going anywhere,
I will be their mother, and father as well.
I will hold up strong, try not to do wrong.
I will make them proud, and they will shout it aloud.

Sour and Sweet

Life is a source of sour and sweets.
As sour as you feel now,
Sweeter days will come,
Then delightful, exquisite nights.
As weak as you may feel,
Know that you have stronger and more rightful days ahead of you.
You are not alone at this time of great sorrow,
As you have God to guide you through life,
Regardless of the darkest lanes and narrow roads.

Same Inside

Did my ears deceive me...?
Let me rewind my brain to retrieve her words.
I was wrong,
I heard her right.
How can she hate the Colour of my skin?
What's in a Colour, to make her feel peevish…?
If she was in danger, and only could be saved
By a person of the same Colour as I, then what?
Would she refuse their help because of their Colour?
Moreover, would she be willing to leave behind…
Her father, mother and child rather than accept help from a person of Colour?
Those words I heard, I could not believe still existed.
What's in a Colour, to make a person's eyes red?
Moreover, not have control over her words?
If there wasn't black, there couldn't be white.
It's as saying there's only morning and no night.
It is not our Colour that makes us achieve greatness, it's our brain,
Furthermore, the information we store in them.
When you look past our colouring, the insides are the same.
Be careful of your words, do not isolate yourself:
There might just be a day when you implore to a person of Colour.

Child Talk

So crucial it is when a child begins to question.
"Why the sky is blue, and you are you?"
He stands up tall, stares straight in your eyes; he is looking for answers to clear his mind.
"Why my skin is brown and known as black, why my brain recalls and mirrors to reflect?"
The questions are hard and answers far to fetch, but do your best not let him down.
His brain is expanding to connect with our world; he is lost in his mind and looking for an exit.
He needs your help to let him out…
Take him by the hand and gently through the steps.
Explain the way the world is…
"Not all has an answer or means to it, but slowly with time your brain will adjust, to understand the whys and won'ts…
Therefore, for now my son, keep your mind at bay and do your best, don't let it go astray".

Faith

Through the darkest door, I see light.
In the saddest room, I am joyful.
The sharper the words, the blunter the effect.
The longer the road, the quicker I reach.
The darker the dream, I still wake refreshed.
The deeper my faith is, the stronger I am.

Royal Me

It is dangerous when we are together…
Passions of flame, that burns with desire and lust.
The tingles I feel, I cannot describe.
The pleasure I receive, grows uncontrolled.
O how divine… what a night it was.
My mind loses all sense of the world,
I don't want it to end.
It should always be like this.
Nights of passion and days of pleasure,
Day after day, I would be queen of my castle,
Moreover, he will be my golden treasure.

Invisible Friend

You sweetened my life with your presence,
You empowered me with your voice
That carried no judgement in its tone.
You were the figure I never dreamed, but was grateful to have had.
You taught me many things;
This makes me the person I am.
You reasoned wisely, and lifted my doubts,
You were a gift in my life,
I felt safe with you around.
You were poised,
This kept you in with the trend.
You are not around, still,
You remain in my life…
You are my invisible friend.

In Your Space

Before you go, leave your footprints uncovered.
Therefore, I may walk in their tracks and pick up where you left off,
I will finish what you started.
With all the praise I will put in your name.

Your efforts will not have been in vain,
Your debts will be regained.
When the time comes and you are beamed to the sky…
Your empire will be many stories high.

Your loved ones will be cared for.
They will not be homeless, nor rejected.
Therefore, worry not; keep bright your thoughts.

Remember

You will remember me.
All the days I cried and moaned from the pain you caused me, you will remember me.
All the shouting, punching and biting at me like a wild dog on a leash, you will remember me.
The spitting, and twitching, the vicious words that rolled off your tongue, as though of a serpent snake, you will remember me.
You will not sleep in peace, you will not be at ease, you will remember, but then it will be too late.
Too late to turn back the clock, and reform your words.
Too late to hold back your hands, and too late to take in what you spat out.
You will remember me for my weakness, for being at your mercy, and the courage it took to break away from you.

Precious Tears

Do not share those tears girl, wipe your eyes.
Wipe the stains that stream your face,
You are better than that girl, stronger than you think.

Open your eyes don't blur them out,
Stop hiding behind the liquid that fills the lids of your eyes.
Blink them out and dry them clean, you are better than that.

If you could escape from that empty shell you call your body,
You could see your real self.

The beautiful you, that is loved and adored by most.
Not you, that's suppressed and hated by one.
You are you,
Love yourself.

Left Alone

I am here.
I am all alone.
Nowhere to turn
You get on with life.
You think of yourself, leaving no thought for me.
I need your help.

You make me out to be as mighty as the thunder,
You push me in the front line, and hide behind my back.
You think I can do it all.
But I have fear.
I need your help.

I'm all braved-out.
I'm cried-out too.
I have no more strength; I need some of yours,
We are in this together.
I need your help.

You promised you would be here.
But you are always there.
I can't do this myself.
I can't do it anymore.
Come and be by my side,
I need your help.

Courage

Do not lose hope,
There is no shame in wishing you had more than you do.
Your time will come.
You will reap what you sow…
I share your sadness, I feel your desperation.
It shall end, your strength and courage will be sure of it.
You have done wonders for others… helped with their needs.
Now you have a need of your own.
The usual faces have vanished, not around to help ease your burden.
I understand your discontent, and fury,
However, don't lose hope; be strong
For your time is coming.
It is creeping, rather than running, but it is coming.

You Say You Care

Did you find the joy you seek
When you said his love for me is fake,
Furthermore, my heart he will break?

Did you reach your targeted goal
When you wished he would leave me alone?

Did it not matter to you, that in him, I planted my love?
And wanted no other, but him?
You knew I came from far, and when I reached,
I gave my all!
What effort would it have taken
To neither stand aside nor intervene?

Language of the heart belongs to its speakers,
Not visitors who don't understand.

I respect your views, I understand you care.
However, where my heart is concerned, I wish you can
Leave be, because I can take care.

I Forgave You

You stood in the way of my happiness,
My destiny and anything decent I aimed for-
You taunted me with your tongue, so bitter even
Your teeth could not imprison.
Now you ask for my forgiveness.

Well, I do. I forgave you long before now.

I never was scared of your words.

I pitied you. I pitied the fact that you
Thought of me as competition you needed to destroy.

I grudged you not. I overlooked your shallowness.
You were no object in my path,
For I have encountered and overcome many obstacles.
You were no match for me.

Learn the Lesson

Run with the wind instead of running with your thoughts,
Free yourself of your past, and look ahead.
You once did wrong, back then you were young.
He fooled your mind, and took for granted your heart.
Don't beat yourself up, for what has been, and passed.
With every mistake, a lesson is there to learn.
With every lesson, wisdom is there to gain.
Omit your past, its time has gone… move on to hold times to come.

Memories

Memories of my days of youth filled with hurt and pain.
Hurt from the cruel laughter of kids pointing and sniggering at my difference to them.
Hurt so strong that it pounded my delicate heart with rhythms and beats like a steel band's on a hot summer's day.
Hurt that made my brow fill up with sweat, as if I was in the scorching sun running a race.
Memories of my days of youth, full of sadness, yet I am grateful that I have lived.
I have lived through it all, and now I am stronger than most who sniggered and laughed; and I am here to tell my tale.

Transformation

A gullible young creature, I once had been,
I hid behind the crowd too shy to speak.
Always ready to please, just to be accepted.
Hated to disappoint, in case I was denied.
I did not speak much, mostly hushed my mouth.
I was not sure of what to say, mostly silenced my thoughts.

Now look at me, the transformation I have made.

My brain works over-time.
My mouth runs non-stop.
In crowds, I feel free to express myself.
The shyness… still there a little
Nevertheless; gullible I am no more.

True Friend

Feelings of disappointment rained over me as she muttered, "You were not a true friend."
How after all these years has she come up with such a conclusion?
She was my other half, partner in crime. She had no shadow because I was in her shadow's place.
We laughed, we sang, we danced around.
When things got bad, we even cried together.
All the lying I have done for her, she has never done for me. All the sneaking around I sneaked for her, she never sneaked for me.
When I felt worthless, troubled and friendless, where was my dear friend?
I found her with the rest laughing at my distress. Therefore, how can she feel I am not a true friend?
I need not say, I was the true friend, not her.

In Search of a Way

I shout because I am scared… and confused as well.
Your battle is hard… but I have fought worse.
Life is what we make of it, so show me the result.
I have sweated and bled, where is my reward?
I want to give up, cannot go on any further.

The good always suffer before they make it…

I have suffered enough and am nowhere near the finish line.
When will my time come? When will I rejoice?
I have waited far long.
Show me the corner to turn, to grab my fortune.

My Heart's Key

You have waited for a while; now put out your hand,
Take hold of the key.

With this key, you have permission to enter my heart.
Beware of the signs; they are there for a reason.

The sign on the left shows the amount of times it's been abandoned
…left stranded.
The sign on the right indicates its purity, but yet wrongful
Treatments it has received.
At the top in that small space, that is where my hope sleeps.

Now look down at the bottom of my heart,
In the never-ending vanity bag; there you will find
Dusts of love, which trickle out with every step I take.

Right in the centre is my safety place, where my key belongs.
If the time comes, and you wish to leave, be sure to
Replace my key in its proper place before you exit.

Holding On

Delightful sensations I feel, he will be mine all night.
'To have and to hold', words so strong,
I felt at that moment, our love began to unfold.
'For richer or poorer' we will clutch on tight,
Indeed our faith will see us right.
Regardless of the differences we have,
My love is the keeper of my heart.
For he is my man, and I am his woman.

Changes

You are not as I remembered you to be.
Your glow that could stop me in my tracks has faded with time,
Now you are a stranger to me.
Your velvet voice that you once had,
Now screeches non-stop, irritating my ears.
You were my idol. I put you high on a pedestal,
However, you frowned at me.
You thought of yourself as the world,
You had no time for me, but now look; the table has turned.
You see me in a different light. I do you, too.
My focus and energy are elsewhere.

What is it he Sees?

Locked in my thoughts not a sound I could hear, then suddenly a shadow blocked the dazzling sun that shone on me. With a quick glance, I saw the brown chocolate-skinned man who would be my life for many years to come. With a gentle smile, he nodded down at the empty seat beside me, to ask for my approval to sit with me. I of all people, his looks alone made me quiver inside, for I look as boring as a plank of wood. He saw something in me that I did not see and still do not. What is it that he sees?

Another She

Our sudden uncontrollable departure laid him in the arms of a stranger, who just so happened to ease him of the incessant urges that he had felt for me for many months.
I was on the other side of the world. What was I to do, to ease my love of his pain?
I was helpless, so my love turned to the next female he laid his eyes on.
The pain in my heart at the thought of his body linking so closely to another woman feels like either side of my heart had its own weightlifter,
Firmly holding on to its tender corners and slowly but happily ripping apart this delicate part of my inside, causing me agony to feel every inch of its tear.
Was our love that weak?
It had just been a few months, and already he was in the arms of another woman? How could I share my uneasy trouble with anyone?
He was as perfect as a rainbow on a rainy day, not a foot he could put wrong; so who would believe my yarn of this faultless man without hearing my tale straight out of the horse's mouth?

Used

Hope you felt good when you spoilt my mood.
With no proof, you caved in the roof.
Were you there to impress them?
With no regret, you chucked me in the pool, pool of shame without a shallow end.
How hollow can one be?
You twisted my words and reshaped their framing.
I was your friend when you had none.
How disheartening to know that I have been used and abused;
However, all is well.
I will go on with my head held high.
Because I was a good friend, and that you cannot deny.

You Changed

We fell for each other,
For everything, we did together.
Our sprits linked.
We became incomplete apart.
You were my best friend,
All I ever wanted.

We knew our ins and outs...
You started a sentence,
I finished your sentence.
Our highs and lows, we shared,
However, your money you kept, then
You stretched your hand, and mine you took.

You changed before my eyes,
You shattered the love we had.

Thoughts

You were born alone,
Therefore, live your life to the fullest,
Your mind is your own,
You are your mind.
Say what you think,
Reduce your brain's overload.
Do what you want,
Except, there may be consequences.
Remember, you control your mind,
Do not allow your mind to control you.

God's Gift

Twenty-four years young, three kids while I am strong.
For the life I give, I find not wrong.
They are my strength when I am weak,
They are my courage that I seek.
They are the push that I feel when I want to give up.
They are my gifts from God, not one but three.

A Day at the Fair

A day at the fair brought back a feeling I have not felt for a while. The warm breeze that blew in my face reminded me of a time I had long forgotten.

I braced myself and sat in the metal seat of the roller coaster. With a sudden slam, the door shut and trapped me like a caged bird. Too late to change my mind now so I just relaxed and let the turning of the big wheel swing me from a side to side. Before I knew it, the wind had lifted me off the ground. The mightiness of the gust gushed in my face, drying up my mouth, and I let out a scream as mighty as the wind to release me of the tension that had built in me for a very long time. I felt young and free again, but that just lasted for five minutes. Five sweet minutes I would give anything to have again. Those tiny minutes were mine, mine to have, and to hold, and I do. I hold them locked in my mind.

Woman with Child

Woman with child full of grace and peace,
Woman with child so delicately at ease,
Woman with child anxiously awaits,
Woman with child counting down the days,
Woman with child sensitively asleep.

Days upon days cannot get any rest.
Days upon days tired and stress.

Her unborn child so delicate and soft,
Her unborn child wiggles and squirms,
Her unborn child has no place to turn.

Woman and child look forward to meeting,
Woman and child struggles through the pain,
Woman and child the day is here,
Woman and child prepare to greet,
Woman and child at last they are free.

Mother says to her child, "thank God you are here".
Mother looks at her child, unable to control herself, weeps.
Mother and child caress and sleep.

A New World

My past world, crammed with wrong-doers.
Now my world
Taken over with vipers of their own sense.
Vipers who pray on our youths like scavengers,
They leave them with little of a life, or none.

Their mothers left mystified, and their fathers,
Only cry like the days they were born.

There have been many great dreamers in my past world.
With some lived and gone, now their dreams come
Out of dreamland only half fulfilled.

I too, sleep and dream that one day my children,
With their children yet to come, will live in unity.
Furthermore, the vipers of my world will be no more.

It will delight me in every way to hear
Laughter of my children and their children,
Echoing in this new world.

Even if I am no longer in existence, I will be proud.
Furthermore, privileged, that my children and their offspring
Live on in a better world, fearless and free.

Ending

It has ended, so farewell my friend.
The sparks died between us, let's not pretend.
Everything has its moment.
What we pursued was not of intent.
Look back not with regret.
However, move forward and reflect.
We cannot live in a lie and pretend my friend,
Therefore, take care to the end.

Printed in the United Kingdom by
Lightning Source UK Ltd., Milton Keynes
139699UK00001B/152/P

9 781440 120046